Parent's Introduction

We Both Read is the first series of books designed to invite parents and children to share the reading of a story by taking turns reading aloud. This "shared reading" innovation, which was developed with reading education specialists, invites parents to read the more complex text and storyline on the left-hand pages. Then, children can be encouraged to read the right-hand pages, which feature less complex text and storyline, specifically written for the beginning reader.

Reading aloud is one of the most important activities parents can share with their child to assist them in their reading development. However, We Both Read goes beyond reading *to* a child and allows parents to share the reading *with* a child. *We Both Read* is so powerful and effective because it combines two key elements in learning: "modeling" (the parent reads) and "doing" (the child reads). The result is not only faster reading development for the child, but a much more enjoyable and enriching experience for both!

You may find it helpful to read the entire book aloud yourself the first time, then invite your child to participate in the second reading. In some books, a few more difficult words will first be introduced in the parent's text, distinguished with **bold lettering**. Pointing out, and even discussing, these words will help familiarize your child with them and help to build your child's vocabulary. Also, note that a "talking parent" icon 🗪 precedes the parent's text and a "talking child" icon 🗪 precedes the child's text.

We encourage you to share and interact with your child as you read the book together. If your child is having difficulty, you might want to mention a few things to help them. "Sounding out" is good, but it will not work with all words. Children can pick up clues about the words they are reading from the story, the context of the sentence, or even the pictures. Some stories have rhyming patterns that might help. It might also help them to touch the words with their finger as they read, to better connect the voice sound and the printed word.

Sharing the *We Both Read* books together will engage you and your child in an interactive adventure in reading! It is a fun and easy way to encourage and help your child to read—and a wonderful way to start them off on a lifetime of reading enjoyment!

We Both Read: We All Sleep

We Both Read® is a trademark of Treasure Bay, Inc.

Published by Treasure Bay, Inc.
40 Sir Francis Drake Boulevard
San Anselmo, CA 94960 USA

Printed in Singapore

Library of Congress Catalog Card Number: 2008930801

Hardcover ISBN-10: 1-60115-235-3
Hardcover ISBN-13: 978-1-60115-235-0
Paperback ISBN-10: 1-60115-236-1
Paperback ISBN-13: 978-1-60115-236-7

We Both Read® Books
Patent No. 5,957,693

Visit us online at:
www.webothread.com

We All Sleep

By D. J. Panec

Illustrated by Gloria Lapuyade

TREASURE BAY

In hopes they will spy a small worm from the sky, the birds are all flying and soaring up **high**.

Are the birds flying down low?

No, the birds are flying up . . .

. . . high!

The sun disappears as it sets in the west.
It's time for some **sleep**. Yes, we all need to rest.

For people and animals, **sleep** is the key.
The birds even **sleep** in their nest in the tree.

Shhh! The birds are . . .

. . . sleeping!

They roll in the **dirt**, as they're playing all day.
These pigs were once pinkish, but now they're more gray.

Are these pigs clean?

No, these pigs are **dirty**!

These pigs are so dirty and really a sight!
I just hope they bathe before bedtime tonight!

Do you think he washed there, in back of his ear?
They're **sleeping** right now, so let's not get too near.

Shhh! The pigs
are **sleeping**!

The cubs that are wrestling are so very **small**.
But soon they will grow into bears that are tall.

Are the bear cubs big?

No, the bear cubs are **small**!

The **bears** like to hibernate all winter long.
To wake them up early would surely be wrong.

Come spring they will rise and find something to eat.
Perhaps now they're dreaming of honey, so sweet.

Shhh! The **bears** are sleeping!

These kittens are curious! Look how they try,
to catch anything that is **fast** or that flies.

Are the kittens slow?

No, the kittens are **fast**!

I don't think the **kittens** will catch that quick mouse.
Let's hope as they chase, they do not wreck the house!

Oh, look at them now, as they lie in the sun!
A short little nap, before having more fun.

Shhh! The **kittens** are sleeping!

These penguins all live in a place that is **cold**.
It snows and it's icy all year, I am told.

Are the penguins hot?

No, the penguins are **cold**!

The **penguins** will slide on the snow and then dive.
They swim like the fish, which they eat to survive.

At night they will huddle in groups to stay warm.
With clouds in the sky, they all know it might storm.

Shhh! The **penguins** are sleeping!

The legs on a rabbit can help it to hop.
They land with a thump, as their **long** ears go flop.

Are the rabbit's ears short?

No, the rabbit's ears are **long**.

Some **rabbits** are pets and some others are wild.
The one with the itch, I am sure he just smiled.

They sleep in their burrows, deep under the ground.
So no one will hear them, they make not a sound.

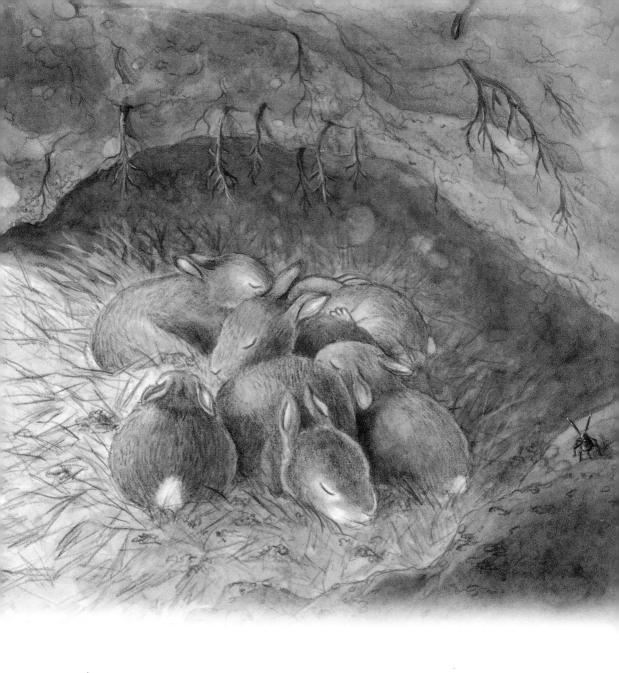

Shhh! The **rabbits** are sleeping!

Most puppies are friendly and love to play tug,
To make them feel **happy**, just give them a hug!

Are these puppies sad?

No, these puppies are **happy**!

They'll jump and they'll yelp and they'll run 'til they drop.
I'm not sure they'll hear, if you ask them to stop.

But when the sun sets, little **puppies** will yawn.
Just watch as they curl up and doze until dawn.

Shhh! The **puppies** are sleeping!

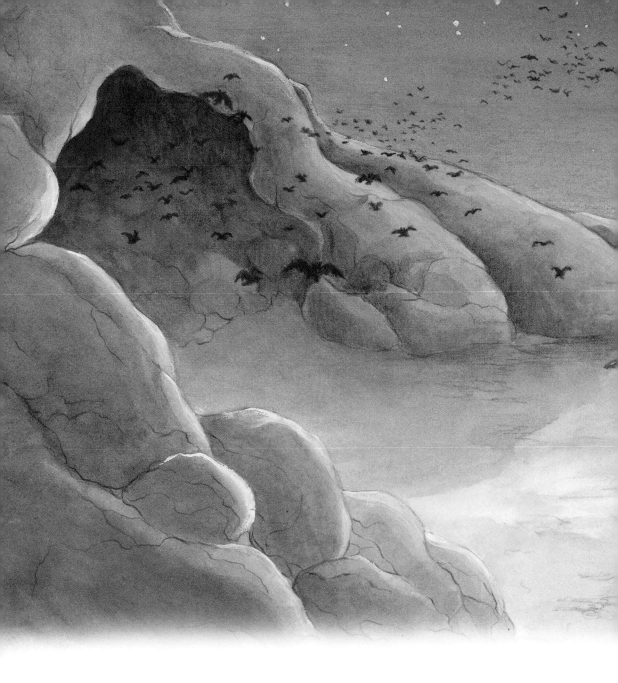

The bats like to sleep in the daytime, I've heard, and wake up at **night**, when they fly like a bird.

Do bats fly during the day?

No, bats fly during the **night**.

Bats eat hoards of insects. This helps us a lot, since too many bugs are too many to swat!

Their feeding's all done; now the **bats** fly back home. They'll sleep upside down in a deep cavern's dome.

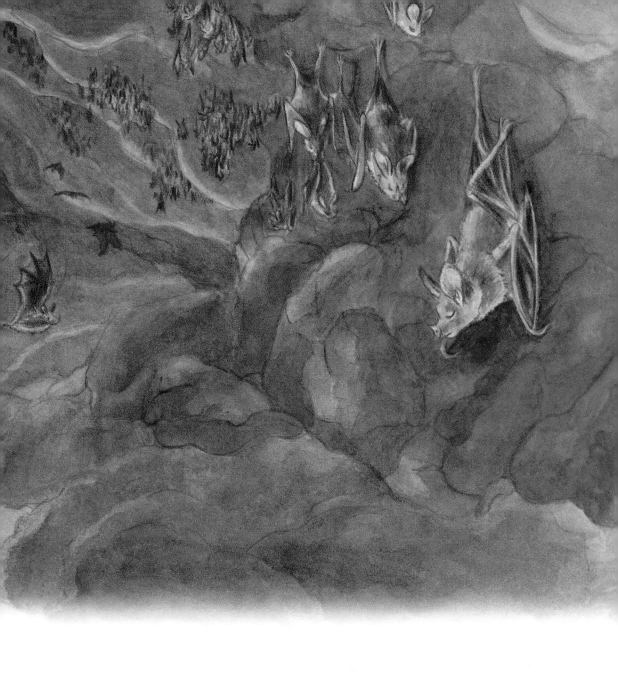

Shhh! The **bats** are sleeping!

The baby tries walking, then falls in the dirt.
His cry is so **loud** that my ears start to hurt!

Is the baby quiet?

No, the baby is **loud**!

The **baby** makes sounds, but he really can't talk.
He takes little steps as he's learning to walk.

But now he is tired and lies in my lap.
Let's be very quiet and just let him nap.

Shhh! The **baby** is sleeping.

You make it seem **easy**! You're reading so fine!
Yes, soon you will read all of your part and mine.

Is reading this book hard?

No, reading this book is **easy**!

We're both a bit tired, I think you'll agree,
but **I am** so glad you have read this with me.

Your eyes are so droopy, it's hard to ignore.
In one minute more, you'll be starting to snore!

Shhh! **I am** sleeping.

If you liked **We All Sleep,** here is another
We Both Read® Book you are sure to enjoy!

Just Five More Minutes!

It's Mark's bedtime, but he begs his mom for "just
five more minutes"! When his five minutes are
up, he keeps coming up with more things to do
that will take him "just five more minutes". Each
new thing is more funny and outlandish than the
last, including teaching a dinosaur how to tie his
shoes and brushing George Washington's teeth on
Mount Rushmore!